JUNIOR GEOLOGIST

Discovering Rocks, Minerals, and Gems

WHAT IS SOIL?

JOE GREEK

Britannica Educational Publishing

IN ASSOCIATION WITH

ROSEN

EDUCATIONAL SERVICES

Published in 2016 by Britannica Educational Publishing (a trademark of Encyclopædia Britannica, Inc.) in association with The Rosen Publishing Group, Inc.
29 East 21st Street, New York, NY 10010

Distributed exclusively by Rosen Publishing.
To see additional Britannica Educational Publishing titles, go to rosenpublishing.com.

First Edition

Britannica Educational Publishing
J.E. Luebering: Director, Core Reference Group
Mary Rose McCudden: Editor, Britannica Student Encyclopedia

Rosen Publishing
Hope Lourie Killcoyne: Executive Editor
Tracey Baptiste: Editor
Nelson Sá: Art Director
Nicole Russo: Designer
Cindy Reiman: Photography Manager
Tracey Baptiste: Photo Researcher

Library of Congress Cataloging-in-Publication Data

Greek, Joe, author.
What is soil? / Joe Greek. – First edition.
pages cm. – (Junior geologist: discovering rocks, minerals, and gems)
Audience: Grades 1 to 4.
Includes bibliographical references and index.
ISBN 978-1-68048-246-1 (library bound) – ISBN 978-1-5081-0051-5 (pbk.) – ISBN 978-1-68048-304-8 (6-pack)
1. Soils–Juvenile literature. 2. Soil formation–Juvenile literature. 3. Soil ecology–Juvenile literature. I. Title.
S591.3.G74 2016
551.3–dc23

201

Manufactured in the United States of America

Photo credits: Cover, p. 1 nito/Shutterstock.com; cover and interior pages background Vitaly Korovin/Shutterstock.com; p. 4 Johanna Photolibrary/Getty Images; p. 5 Dougal Waters/Digital Vision/Getty Images; p. 6 Leonello Calvetti/Science Photo Library/Getty Imag Dave Yoder/National Geographic Magazines/Getty Images; p. 8 Martin Shields/Science Source/Getty Images; p. 9 David Hill/Photolil Getty Images; p. 10 Timothy O'Keefe/Photolibrary/Getty Images; p. 11 Grant Dixon/Lonely Planet Images/Getty Images; p. 12 Jim Richardson/National Geographic Image Collection/Getty Images; p. 13 Encyclopaedia Britannica, Inc.; p. 14 DonNichols/E+/Getty In p. 15 Dan Brownsword/Cultura/Getty Images; p. 16 Yasuhide Fumoto/DigitalVision/Getty Images; p. 17 Robb Kendrick/National Gec Magazines/Getty Images; p. 18 © Santiago Urquijo/Moment/Getty Images; p. 19 Luc Hoogenstein/Buiten-beeld/Minden Pictures/Ge Images; p. 20 Brent Stirton/Stone/Getty Images; p. 21 Martin Harvey/Digital Vision/Getty Images; p. 22 Wally Eberhart/Visuals Unlim Getty Images; p. 23 Scimat Scimat/Science Source/Getty Images; p. 24 Philippe Marion/Moment/Getty Images; p. 25 Michael Christo Brown/National Geographic Magazines/Getty Images; p. 26 Image Source/Getty Images; p. 27 © iStockphoto.com/Roel Smart; p. 28 Imagery/Moment/Getty Images; p. 29 Alexander W Helin/Moment/Getty Images; interior pages (arrow) Mushakesa/Shutterstock.co

JUNIOR GEOLOGIST

Discovering Rocks, Minerals, and Gems

WHAT IS SOIL?

JOE GREEK

Britannica Educational Publishing

CONTENTS

The Soil Beneath Your Feet	4
What Is Soil Good For?	6
How Soil Is Made	8
The Layers of Soil	12
The Need for Topsoil	14
Creatures in the Soil	18
The Colors of Soil	20
Soil Textures	22
Natural Changes	24
Pollution and Soil	26
Taking Care of the Soil	28
Glossary	30
For More Information	31
Index	32

THE SOIL BENEATH YOUR FEET

You may not think much about the dirt beneath your feet, but it is necessary for most life on Earth. Soil provides a place for plants to grow. Plants obtain food and water from the soil. Animals need plants for food and for the oxygen we need to breathe.

Soil is also home to many creatures. Some are large, and others are so small you need a microscope to see them.

Soil gives us much of what we need to live. Most plants, including the food we eat, grow in the soil.

Not only do some soils look different, some are better for growing plants than others.

These creatures are all part of an ecosystem that keeps soil, plants, and animals healthy.

Soil looks and feels different depending on where you are. There are more than 70,000 types of soil in the United States alone! It takes hundreds of years to make soil. Sadly, it can be damaged very quickly.

Compare and Contrast

Think about the soil you might find in a desert and the soil you might find on a farm. How are they different?

WHAT IS SOIL GOOD FOR?

Most life on Earth needs soil to survive. Plants need soil to hold them in place and to provide food. Soil contains nutrients for plants. These are food substances

The roots of a plant hold it in the soil and keep it from falling over.

Think About It

Plants need water and nutrients found in soil to live. Can you think of places where it may be hard for plants to survive?

that help plants grow. Soil also holds water that is absorbed by the roots. Without soil, plants could not survive. Because plants give off the oxygen we need to breathe, we could not survive without soil either!

Plants, such as grass, help prevent the top layer of soil from being washed away by water or blown away by wind. Not all soils can support a large amount of plant life. In deserts—where most plants cannot grow—sandstorms frequently reshape the land.

Hills of sand, known as dunes, are formed by winds that move sand particles around the desert.

HOW SOIL IS MADE

Five major factors control how soil is made. The first is the parent materials. These are basic **minerals** and organic matter—remains of plants and animals. The minerals come from rocks that have broken into tiny pieces over time. These tiny pieces, or particles, are called regolith.

Vocabulary

Minerals make up Earth's rocks, sands, and soils. They are not organic substances. This means that they do not come from an animal or a plant.

Minerals and organic matter are the basic ingredients of soils.

Weathering is another force that creates soil. This happens when forces like wind or rain break minerals into regolith. These forces also carry bits of soil and other particles from one place to another. It can take millions of years for a stony surface to be broken down by weathering.

Climate is another strong force that affects how quickly or slowly soil is formed. Warmer temperatures and high levels of water can speed up the

Ocean waves and sea breezes help form the shape of coastal areas and beaches.

Weathering removes soil from hills and mountains, which can make amazing shapes and formations.

process. Cooler temperatures and less water can slow down the formation of soil.

Land surface features, such as hills and valleys, also affect how soils develop. Soils in high, steep areas, like mountains, form slower than those in low, flat areas. This is because steep slopes are more

Think About It

How fast soil is made depends on several factors, including weathering, climate, and land height. How fast do you think soil in your area was made?

Plant roots can grow above the ground, going around and even through objects like rocks.

exposed to weathering forces that remove soil as it forms.

Plants and animals also affect soil formation. Soil is enriched by absorbing wastes and decaying animals. Plant roots can also grow into cracks found in rocks and break them into smaller pieces.

THE LAYERS OF SOIL

There are four different layers of soil. Each layer is called a horizon. The top layer is very thin. It is made up of humus which is living and dead leaves, plants, and bugs. The soil is very dark in this layer.

Vocabulary

Humus is a dark, organic material that is rich in nutrients. It is formed when plant and animal matter decay.

The roots of small plants like flowers and weeds grow in the topsoil.

Just beneath this layer is topsoil. It also has nutrients, and it holds the roots of smaller plants.

The next layer of soil is the ground layer. It is called subsoil. Subsoil contains mostly minerals and a small amount of humus. Only the deepest plant roots, such as trees, can reach the subsoil.

The fourth layer is called the regolith. This layer is made up of broken rock. Very little organic material is found in this layer. It is also too deep for plant roots.

Beneath the regolith is solid rock. This is called bedrock.

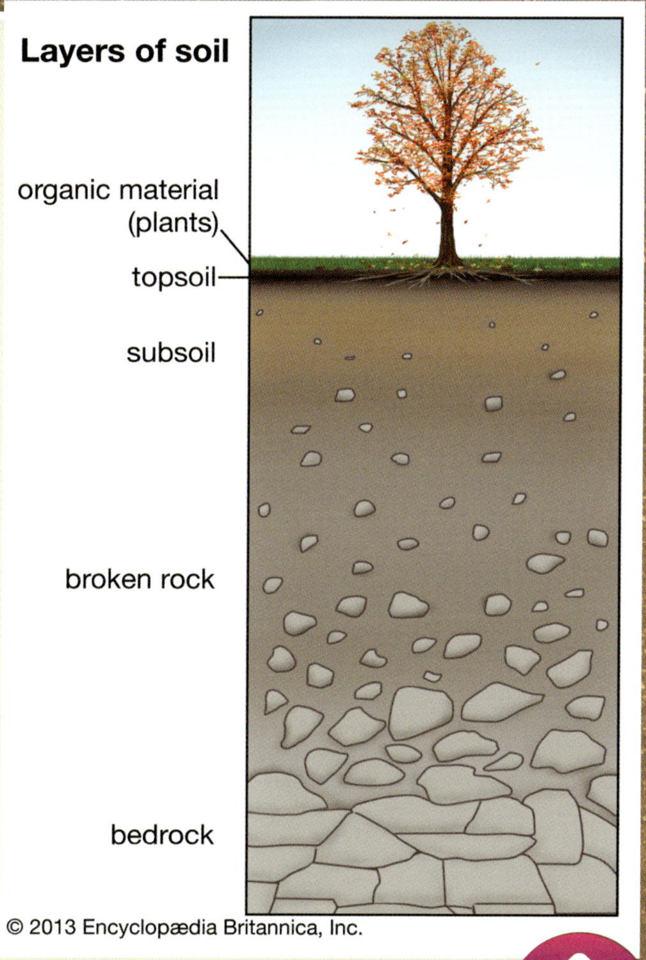

This diagram shows the four layers of soil starting with organic materials at the top. Bedrock is not a soil layer.

THE NEED FOR TOPSOIL

Topsoil is the layer of soil that supports plant life. It is mainly made up of minerals with equal parts water and air and small amounts of organic matter. Near great rivers, the topsoil may be hundreds of feet deep. In most places, however, the topsoil is only about 6 inches (15 centimeters)deep.

Topsoil is the most valuable layer of soil for the survival of animals and humans. Without it, farmers would not be able to grow the food we eat. Animals that only eat plants would quickly starve. Meat-eating animals would also be unable to survive.

Soil that is good for farming is dark and rich in nutrients.

Inside the topsoil, there are small spaces that hold water and air. These spaces are called pores and can be found in the nutrient-rich humus. The pores help keep the soil soft and loose. It is difficult to farm in topsoil that has very little humus.

The amount of humus found in soil can affect how well plants grow.

Compare and Contrast

How is topsoil different from regolith?

Trees change carbon dioxide that comes from the soil into oxygen that we need to breathe.

Air found in topsoil is very different from the air we breathe. Because it is not exposed to moving air, it tends to be very moist. There is also more carbon dioxide than oxygen in topsoil. Over time, the carbon dioxide escapes from the topsoil into the atmosphere. Trees and other plants turn carbon dioxide into the oxygen people breathe.

New topsoil is made all the time, but it is a very slow process. It takes between 500 and 1,000 years for 1 inch (2 cm) of topsoil to form.

When farmers overuse the fields in which they grow crops, the soil can become damaged.

While it takes a very long time for topsoil to form, people can destroy it very quickly. Farming the same area of topsoil every year can reduce the amount of nutrients found in it. Governments and soil scientists work together to find ways to protect topsoil.

Think About It

What do you think farmers can do to make sure the soil they use always has a good amount of nutrients?

CREATURES IN THE SOIL

Plants are not the only living things that call the soil their home. Many animals, both small and big, can be found in the ground. Some even make homes underground to stay safe from bigger animals above.

Millions of tiny organisms can be found in a spoonful of soil. They are so small that we cannot see them. Scientists have to use microscopes to see and study these organisms.

Think About It

Many creatures that live underground cannot see. How do you think they know where they're going?

Earthworms live in the soil and break down organic matter that plants feed on.

Many creatures, like this mole, spend most of their lives underground.

Some animals that live in the soil are easy to see. Some of these are bugs and insects such as ants and centipedes that spend most of their lives underground. Earthworms and larger creatures such as some reptiles and small mammals also live underground.

THE COLORS OF SOIL

Deserts are not always covered in sand. Some have hard, dry, red top layers of soil.

The color of the soil where you live may be different than in other places. Weather and rain affect the color of the soil in different places.

Red soils can be found in areas that have warm summers and mild to cold winters. These areas also have average amounts of rain. The red color of the soil is caused by the presence of **iron oxides**.

Vocabulary

Iron reacts with oxygen and water in moist air to form **iron oxides**, a powdery substance commonly known as rust.

Without rain, soils can dry up and become cracked on their surface.

Like red soils, yellow soils have iron oxides present. However, yellow soils also contain more water than red soils.

Gray and white soils can be found in places that get very little rain. Without much water to mix with oxygen, iron oxides cannot form. Places like deserts have these types of soil colors.

SOIL TEXTURES

The three types of soil textures *(from left to right)* are sand, loam, and clay.

There are three types of soil textures: clay, sand, and loam. The size of the particles in the soil determines if the texture is smooth or rough. The texture can also tell us how much water the soil can absorb.

Clay soils feel very smooth. Their particles are very small and packed tightly together. Farmers call them heavy soils because it is hard to pull a plow through them. They do not absorb water very well.

When viewed through a microscope, you can see the rough surface of sand particles.

The particles in sand, however, are big. They can be easily seen without a microscope and feel gritty. Particles in sandy soils are loose and do not absorb water well.

The size of particles found in loam soils falls in between those found in clays and sandy soils. They are able to easily absorb and hold water. Most of the world's farming soil is a type of loam.

Think About It

Cacti thrive in sandy soils. With such loose soil, why don't they fall over?

NATURAL CHANGES

Wind, water, and other natural forces cause rocks and soil to wear away. Sometimes the particles that are worn away are carried to another area. These processes are called weathering and erosion. They change the shape of the land.

Wind carries sand and other small bits of earth from one place to another. In dry, sandy areas, this process can constantly create and erode sand dunes. In other places, the changes may take place over longer periods of time. River water

Sand blown by the wind can reshape rocks over long periods of time.

Think About It

The Grand Canyon was created by the flowing water of the Colorado River. What other natural formations do you think were made by wind or water?

picks up and moves mud, pebbles, and larger rocks as it flows downstream. These particles rub against the riverbed and erode, or wear away more rock and soil. When water keeps flowing over one area, it can wear away the rock over a long period of time.

Weathering and erosion can be very harmful to farmland. Crops depend on rich soil for healthy growth, but this top layer of soil is thin. Wind and flowing water can sweep it away.

Flowing rivers can cut into the soil to form deep valleys and canyons.

POLLUTION AND SOIL

Littering, or tossing garbage on the ground, is a form of land pollution. Litter is unpleasant to look at, but, more important, litter can destroy the habitats, or homes, of plants and animals.

Littering is harmful to the environment and can damage soil.

Litter can cover the ground and cut off air and water to animals and plants. Some litter, such as plastics and batteries, contain chemicals that are dangerous. Other chemicals used on the ground by farms and factories, such as **pesticides**, can also be poisonous.

The buildup of dangerous chemicals in the ground is harmful to soil. These chemicals can spread to plants and animals. They may even harm people who eat the contaminated plants and animals.

Chemicals in soil can also spread to nearby water, such as a river. Drinking the polluted water can hurt or kill animals and people.

Vocabulary

Pesticides are chemicals used to kill or repel pests. They are often used to protect crops from insects.

Batteries produce a dangerous chemical that can stay in the soil for a long time.

TAKING CARE OF THE SOIL

While it is a very thin layer of Earth, the soil is very important to life on the planet. Without it, we would not be able to survive. It is everyone's job to take care of the environment, including the soil.

Farmers use several methods to slow down erosion. They plant trees around farmland to block wind. They also cut terraces, or ledges, into sloping land. Water gathers on the terraces rather than rushing down the slope and carrying away the soil.

Terrace farming helps to slow down the effects of erosion.

Compare and Contrast

Many things we throw away can be recycled. Think about the things you throw away at school and at home. What do you think could be used again?

We can all help protect the soil by not littering. By recycling our garbage, such as paper and plastic, we are doing our part to keep the ground and soil clean. When we take care of the soil, we make the world a better and healthier place to live.

The soil helps to protect the surface of Earth. It gives us food to eat and air to breathe.

GLOSSARY

absorb To take in.

atmosphere The layer of gas that surrounds Earth.

carbon dioxide A gas necessary for life on Earth. Animals breathe it out and plants absorb it.

contaminated When something poisonous or unpleasant has been added to something else.

dirt Loose soil or earth.

dune A hill or ridge of sand piled up by the wind.

matter Anything that takes up space.

microscope A tool used by scientists that makes very small objects easier to see.

oxygen A gas necessary for life on Earth. Plants release it and animals breathe it in.

particle A very small piece.

pollution The addition of harmful or poisonous substances to the environment.

pore A tiny opening or space.

recycle To turn waste or garbage into reusable materials or items.

FOR MORE INFORMATION

BOOKS

Aloian, Molly. *Different Kinds of Soil* (Everybody Digs Soil). St. Catharines, ON, Canada: Crabtree Publishing, 2010.

Reilly, Kathleen. *Explore Soil!: With 25 Great Projects* (Explore Your World). White River Junction, VT: Nomad Press, 2015.

Schuh, Mari. *Soil Basics* (Science Builders). Mankato, MN: Capstone Press, 2011.

Silverstein, Alvin, and Virginia Silverstein. *Life in a Bucket of Soil* (Dover Children's Science Books). Mineola, NY: Dover Publications Inc., 2013.

Walker, Sally M. *Studying Soil.* New York, NY: Lerner Publishing, 2013.

WEBSITES

Because of the changing nature of Internet links, Rosen Publishing has developed an online list of websites related to the subject of this book. This site is updated regularly. Please use this link to access the list:
http://www.rosenlinks.com/GEOL/Soil

INDEX

animals
  that live in soil, 4–5, 18–19
  as part of soil, 8, 11

bedrock, 13

carbon dioxide, 16
clay, 22, 23
climate, 9–10, 20

deserts, 7, 21

erosion, 24, 25, 28

farming, 14, 17, 22, 23, 25, 27, 28

gray soils, 21

horizon, 12
humus, 12, 13, 15

iron oxides, 20, 21

littering, 26–27, 29
loam, 22, 23

minerals, 8, 9, 13, 14

nutrients, 6, 12, 13, 15, 17

oxygen, 4, 7, 16

pesticides, 27
plants
need for soil, 4, 5, 6–7, 13
and soil formation, 11, 12
pollution, 26–27, 29
pores, 15

red soils, 20, 21
regolith, 8, 9, 13, 15

sand, 22, 23, 24
soil
  colors of, 20–21
  how it's made, 8–11
  importance of for life, 4–5, 6–7
  layers of, 12–13
  surface features, soil formation and, 10–11
  textures, 22–23
subsoil, 13

topsoil
importance of, 14–17
what it is, 13

weathering, 9, 24–25
white soils, 21

yellow soils, 21